# Suzuki
## Organ School
### Volume 1
*International Edition*

AMPV: 1.00

ISBN-10: 1-4706-4015-5
ISBN-13: 978-1-4706-4015-6

# CONTENTS

# INTRODUCTION

*FOR THE STUDENT:* This material is part of the worldwide Suzuki Method® of teaching. Companion recordings should be used with these publications.

*FOR THE TEACHER:* In order to be an effective Suzuki teacher, a great deal of ongoing education is required. Your regional and/or country Suzuki association provides this for its membership. Teachers are encouraged to become members of their regional or country Suzuki associations and commit to ongoing training via institutes, workshops, and other teacher training programs.

*FOR THE PARENT:* Credentials are essential for any teacher you choose. We recommend you ask your teacher for his or her credentials, especially those relating to training in the Suzuki Method®. The Suzuki Method® experience should be a positive one, where there exists a wonderful, fostering relationship among child, parent, and teacher. Choosing the right teacher is of the utmost importance.

To obtain more information about the Suzuki Association in your region, please contact:

International Suzuki Association USA Office
PO Box 260032
Plano, TX 75026

www.internationalsuzuki.org

# Suzuki Method

## New and Effective Educational Method

Through the experience I have gained by conducting experiments in teaching young children for more than thirty years, I have come to the definite conclusion that musical ability is not an inborn talent but an ability that can be developed. Any child, properly trained, can develop musical ability just as all children in the world have developed the ability to speak their mother tongue. Children learn the nuances of their mother tongue through repeated listening, and the same process should be followed in the development of an ear for music. Children should listen to the recordings of the music that they are studying or about to study every day. This listening helps them to make rapid progress. The children will begin to try their best to play as well as the performer on the recording. By this method the child will grow into a person with fine musical sense. It is the most important training of musical ability.

## Tonalization

The word "tonalization" is a word coined to apply to violin training as an equivalent to vocalization in vocal training. Tonalization has produced wonderful results in violin education. It should be equally effective in all instrumental education. Tonalization is the instruction given the student as he learns each new piece of music, to help him produce a beautiful tone and to use meaningful musical expression. We must train the student to develop a musical ear that is able to recognize a beautiful tone. He must then be taught how to reproduce the beautiful tone and fine musical expression of the artists of the past and present.

## Important Hints in Teaching

### 1. Getting the Student to Enjoy Practicing

What is the best way to get a student to enjoy learning and practicing? This is the principal problem for the teacher and parents – motivating the child properly so that he will enjoy practicing correctly at home. They should discuss this matter together, considering and examining each case in order to help the child enjoy the lessons and practice. Parents and teachers should be sensitive to the feelings of the child. Forcing the child every day saying, "Practice, practice, practice," is the worst method of education and only makes the child hate practicing.

### 2. Having the Child Listen to the Recordings

If, in addition to daily practice at home, the student listens to the recording of the piece he is learning every day and as often as possible, progress will be rapid. Six days a week of practice and listening at home will be more decisive in determining the child's rate of advancement than one or two lessons a week.

### 3. Instruction in Reading Music

The student should always play without music at the lessons. This is the most important factor in improving the student's memory. It also speeds the student's progress. Instruction in music reading should be given according to the student's age and capability. It is very important for the student to learn to read music well, but if the child is forced to read music at the very outset of his study and always practices with music, he will, in performance, feel quite uneasy playing from memory and therefore will not be able to show his full ability.

In acquiring a skill, ability grows through daily practice. In learning his mother tongue, the child begins to read only after he is able to speak. The same approach should be followed in music. Music reading should be taught only after the child's musical sensitivity, playing skill, and memory have been sufficiently trained. It must not be forgotten, however, that reading music is taught in order to be able to play without it. Even after they have acquired the ability to read music, the children as a rule play from memory at all lessons.

## 4. The Educational Method to Develop Ability

When a student gets to the stage where he can play a piece without a mistake in notes or fingering, the time is ripe for cultivating his musicianship. I would say to the child, "Now you are ready. We can start very important work to develop your ability." Then I would proceed to teach a beautiful tone, fine phrasing, and musical sensitivity. The quality of the student's performance depends greatly on the teacher's constant attention to these important musical points.

The following point is very important. When the child can perform piece A satisfactorily and is given a new piece, B, he should not drop A, but practice both A and B at the same time. This procedure should continue as new pieces are added. He should always be reviewing pieces that he knows well in order to develop his ability to a higher degree.

## 5. Private Lessons

Mothers and children should always watch private lessons of other children. This is an added motivation. When the child hears music played well by other children, he will want to be able to play as well, and so his desire to practice will increase.

Lessons should vary in length according to the needs of the child. The attention span of the child should be taken into account. If the small child is able to concentrate for only a short time, it is better to shorten the lesson time. At one time the lesson may be only five minutes, at another, thirty minutes.

Shinichi Suzuki

# Suzuki Method for the Organ

For the first time, young children have the opportunity to learn how to play the church organ. Until now the size of the instrument has prevented children from reaching the pedals. Furthermore, a specially adapted organ-playing method for children had not existed. The authors of this method, Gunilla Rönnberg, Suzuki Organ Teacher and ESA Suzuki Organ Teacher Trainer, and Lars Hagström, organist and organ teacher in Sweden, have, in developing organ teaching according to the Suzuki Method, created a new possibility for young children to play the organ.

## Practice Instruments and Raised Pedals

Lars Hagström has constructed a light, portable practice instrument. This can be adjusted so that children from three years of age, as well as adults, can comfortably reach the pedals. Coordination of the hands and feet is a prerequisite for organ playing. Our teaching of young children has shown us that children achieve this very easily, provided that they start learning at an early age. For church organs there are sets of pedals in two different heights to be put on top of the organ's own pedals. A church organ should always be used in teaching so that the student gets to know the touch of keys and listens to the natural sound of the organ.

## Tonalization

Tonalization is as important on the organ as it is for other instruments. On the organ, it is primarily a combination of attack, release and articulation. The practice of articulation is very important in this method from the very start. Special pedal training is put between other pieces of music in the form of pedal melodies. All pieces otherwise include both pedal and manual playing. When playing the organ the children can experiment with a great choice of registers and sounds.

In our experience, children like to play an instrument with both hands and feet. We are convinced that the organ will be much liked as an instrument for young children to play at an early age.

We would like to thank all who have supported us during the course of developing this material, in particular the Church of Sweden for their financial support.

Gunilla Rönnberg and Lars Hagström

# 1

# Twinkle, Twinkle, Little Star
## Theme
### (non legato)

Teacher may play accompaniment with students for all the Twinkle variations

# Variation A

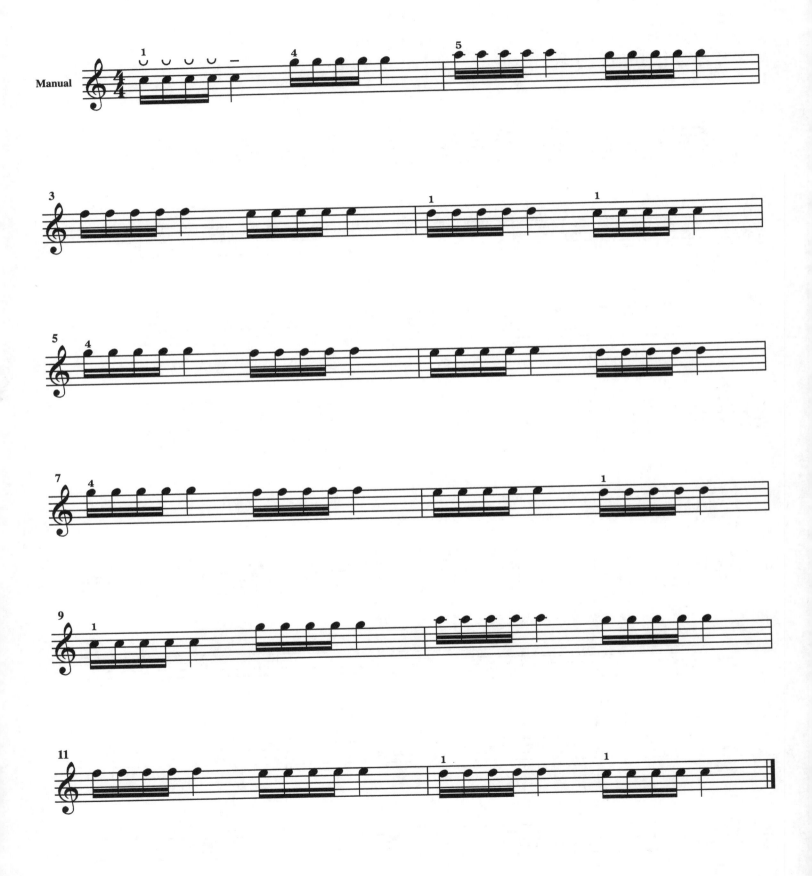

# Variation A

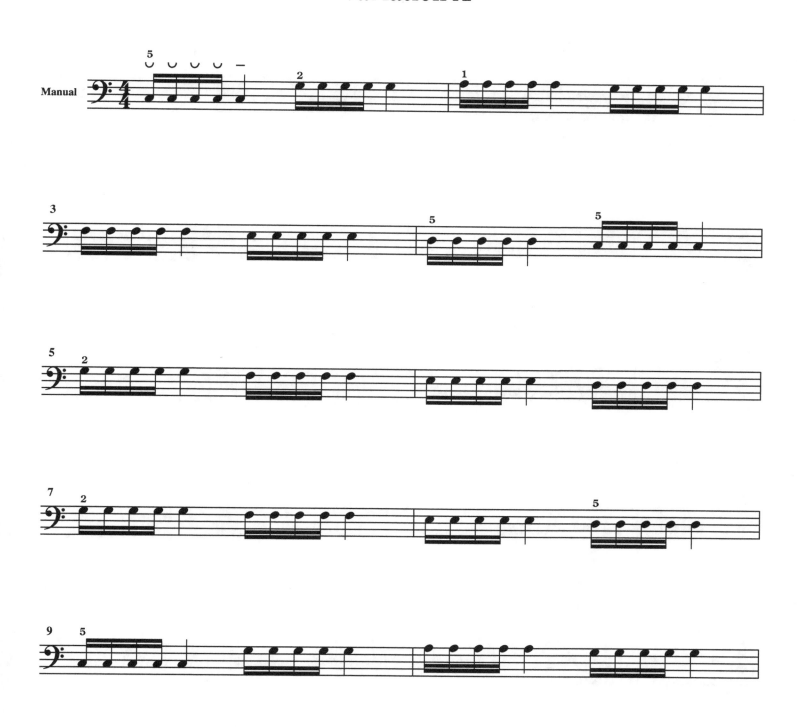

## Variation B

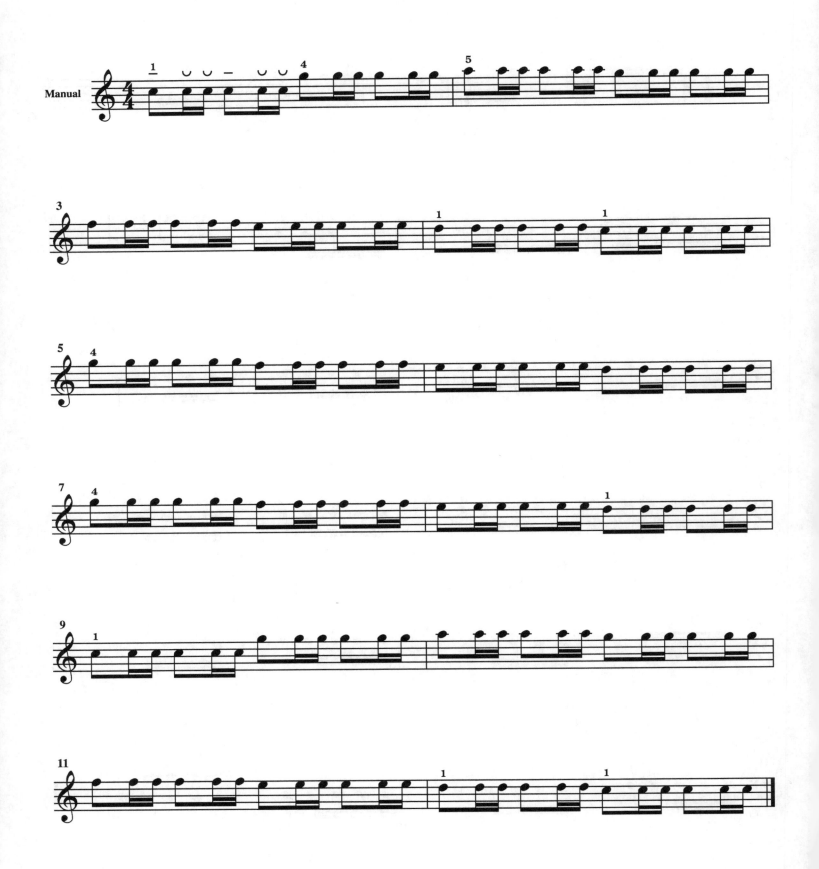

# Variation B

## Variation C

# Theme
## (legato)

# Prepatory Exercise

Registration suggestion:
Principal 4'

Pedal

## 2

# Little Snail
### (legato)

Traditional

Registration suggestion:
Principal 4'

Pedal

5

## 3

# The Fly
### (differentiated non legato)

Traditional

Registration suggestion:
Man I (Gt): Flutes 8', 4'
Ped: 16', 8'

Manual

Pedal

5

Students may also play this piece with the melody in the left hand
( – and ◡ indicate longer and shorter non legato notes)

# Paris
## (legato)

French Folk Song

Registration suggestion:
Principal 4'

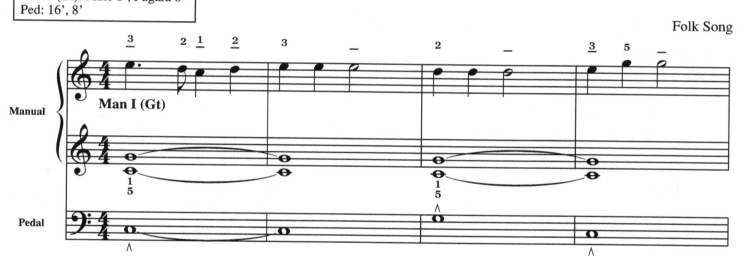

# Mary Had a Little Lamb
## (differentiated non legato)

Registration suggestion:
Man I (Gt): Flute 8', Fugara 8'
Ped: 16', 8'

Folk Song

Students may also play this piece in C-minor

# Piglet

**(legato)**

G. Rönnberg

Registration suggestion:
Stopped diapason 8'
or Prinicipal 4'

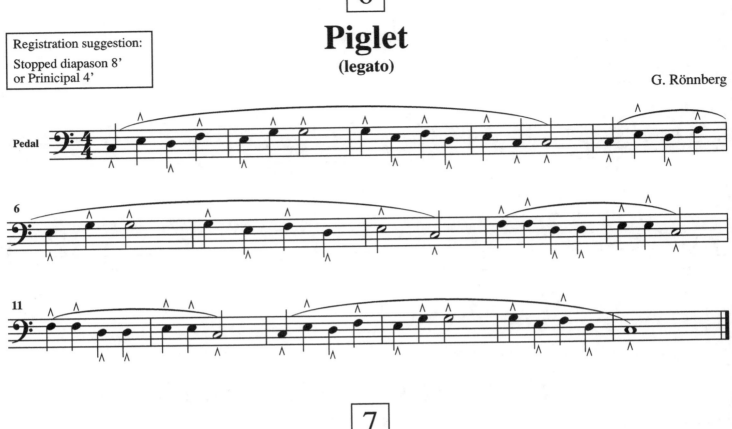

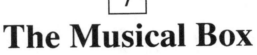

# The Musical Box

**(legato)**

G. Rönnberg

Registration suggestion:
Man I (Gt): Fugara 8', Flute 8'
Ped: 16', 8'

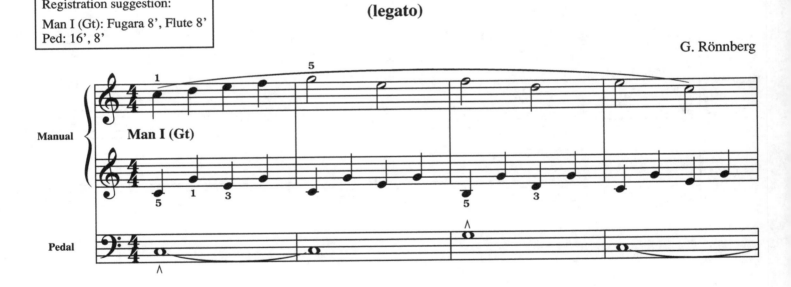

# 8

# Twinkle, Twinkle, Little Star

## Theme
### (non legato)

Registration suggestion:
Principal 4'

## Variation C
### (differentiated non legato)

# 9

# Lightly Row

### (differentiated non legato)

Registration suggestion:

Man I (Gt): Flutes 8', 4'
Ped: 16', 8'

German Folk Song

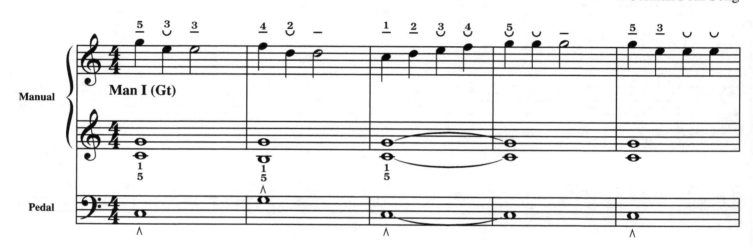

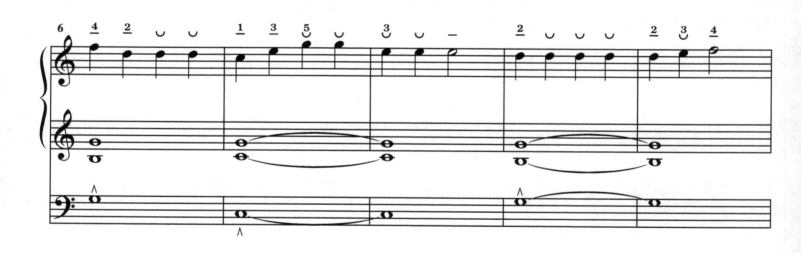

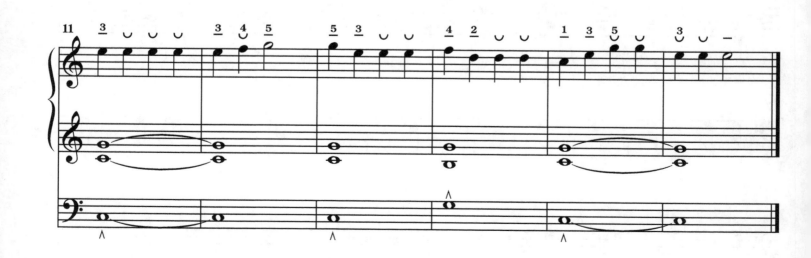

# 10

# A Little Fairytale
## (legato)

G. Rönnberg

Registration suggestion:
Man I (Gt): Stopped diapason 8'
Ped: 16'

Manual

Man I (Gt)

Pedal

# 11

# My School Day
## (differentiated non legato)

Registration suggestion:
Principal 4'

Folk Song

Pedal

## 12

# London Bridge
### (legato)

Registration suggestion:

Man I (Gt): Diapasons 8', 4', 2'
Ped: 16', 8'

English Folk Song

Manual

**Man I (Gt)**

Pedal

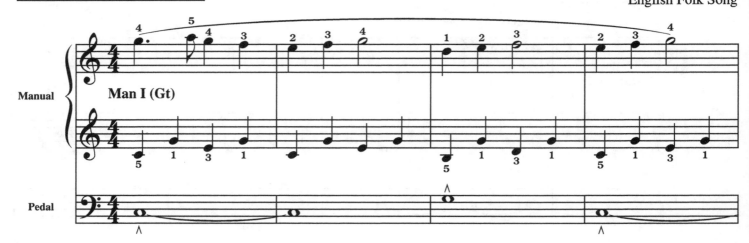

## 13

# Hippopotamus
### (differentiated non legato)

Registration suggestion:

16', 8'

G. Rönnberg

Pedal

# 14

# Cuckoo
**(legato)**

Registration suggestion:
Man I (Gt): Flutes 8', 4'
Ped: 16', 8'

German Folk Song

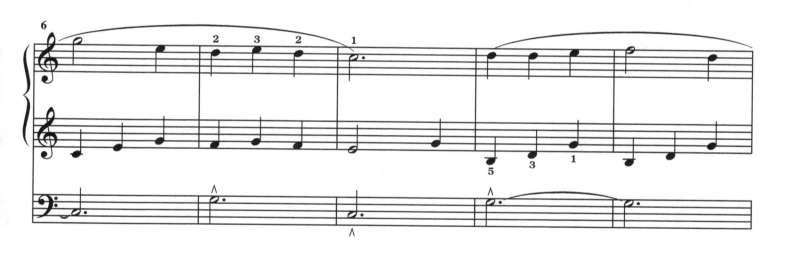

# 15

# Lullaby
## (legato)

German Folk Song

"b" indicates the crossing of one foot behind the other.

# 16

# Amaryllis
## (differentiated non legato)

J. Ghys
arr. G. Rönnberg

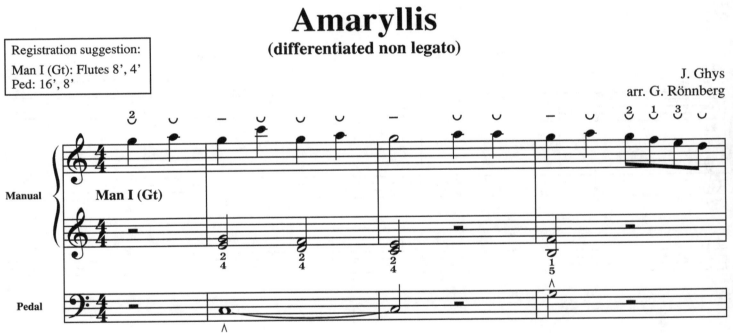

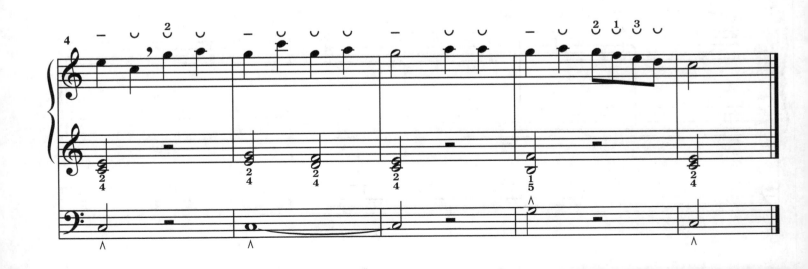

# 19

# Mary Had a Little Lamb

### (differentiated non legato)

Registration suggestion:

Man I (Gt): Soft Flutes or String 8'
Ped: Flute 8' (or Open diapason 8')

Folk Song

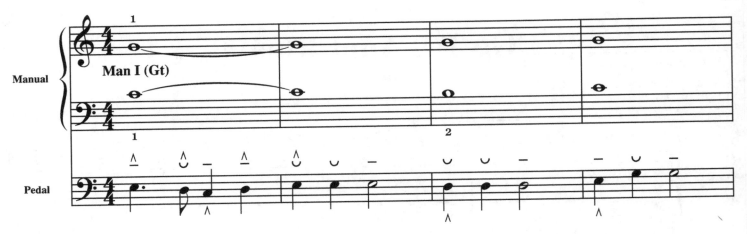

# 20
# Chant Arabe
## (legato)

Registration suggestion:

Man II (Sw): Reed 8' (tremelo ad lib)
Man I (Gt): Flute 8'
Ped: 16'

Anonymous
arr. L. Hagström

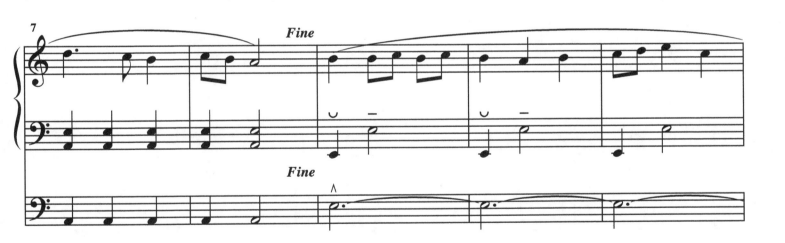

# 25

# Gossip Tune
### (legato)

Registration suggestion:
Principal 4'

German Folk Song

**Pedal**

# 26

# Allegretto
## (legato)

Registration suggestion:

Man I (Gt): Flute 8'
Man II (Sw): Flutes 8', 2'
Ped: 16', 8'

C. Czerny
arr. G. Rönnberg

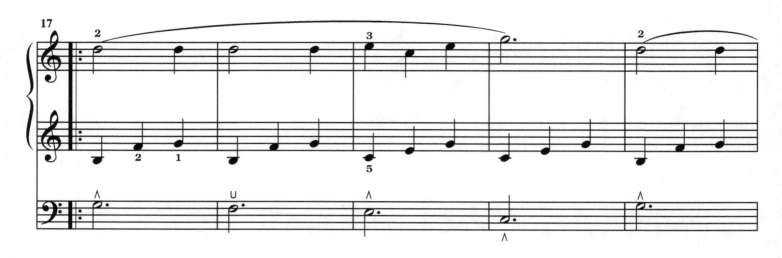